Contents

Being big

Did you know that the biggest living things in the world are trees? Being big is not easy. Big plants and animals have to support their enormous bodies. Big animals have to eat lots of food to survive. And big plants have to pull water up to their leaves, often high above the ground.

The giant sequoia trees of California can grow as high as skyscrapers with over 20 storeys. These trees are so big that cars could drive through a tunnel cut through the trunk!

TRUE or FALSE

A blue whale is too long to fit into an Olympic swimming pool?

Thorny bamboos can grow as tall as 22 people standing on top of each other?

The giant puffball fungus can grow as big as a football?

?

Answers on page 22

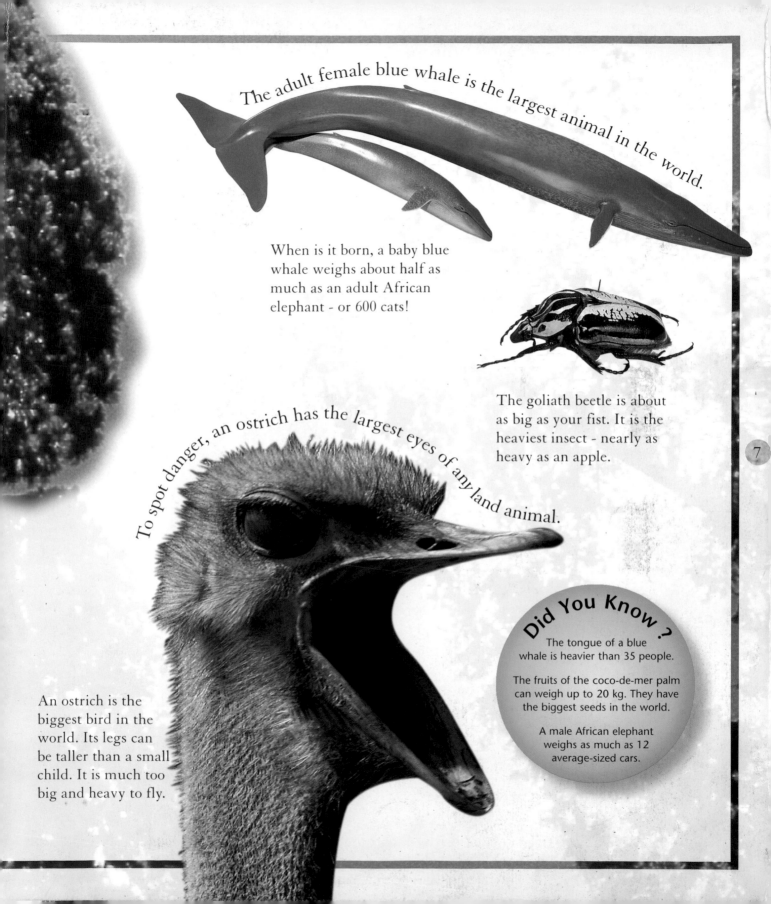

The adult female blue whale is the largest animal in the world.

When is it born, a baby blue whale weighs about half as much as an adult African elephant - or 600 cats!

The goliath beetle is about as big as your fist. It is the heaviest insect - nearly as heavy as an apple.

To spot danger, an ostrich has the largest eyes of any land animal.

An ostrich is the biggest bird in the world. Its legs can be taller than a small child. It is much too big and heavy to fly.

Did You Know ?

The tongue of a blue whale is heavier than 35 people.

The fruits of the coco-de-mer palm can weigh up to 20 kg. They have the biggest seeds in the world.

A male African elephant weighs as much as 12 average-sized cars.

Giant killers

Imagine coming face to face with this tiger! Tigers are one of the biggest killers alive today. Large meat-eaters often have bigger brains than plant-eaters, which help them to plan and carry out their attacks.

Spotty scales lurking in the swamp spell danger.

A tarantula can flick prickly hairs at an enemy.

Bird-eating spiders, or tarantulas, are the biggest spiders, but their poison is less deadly than that of some small spiders, such as black widows.

Green anacondas are the heaviest snakes in the world, and can grow to over nine metres long. They can squeeze a goat to death in their powerful coils.

The Komodo dragon uses its strong toes and sharp claws to tear open and kill deer, wild pigs and water buffalo - sometimes even people! It is the largest lizard in the world.

The ferocious Siberian tiger is the world's biggest cat. It's a deadly hunter, and can eat over 35 kg of meat in just one meal.

Answers on page 22

TRUE
or
FALSE

The enormous basking shark eats people?

A grizzly bear can run after its prey faster than an Olympic sprinter?

An anaconda can kill and eat an elephant?

?

A Siberian tiger has a mighty roar, but it cannot purr.

Water monsters

Water helps to support the weight of plants and animals, and so they can grow larger than those on land. Lurking in the oceans are huge whales, sharks, and crocodiles, as well as squid with gigantic tentacles.

The giant clam is the biggest shellfish. It can grow to over 1 m across, and live for 100 years. Sometimes giant clams grow pearls as big as golf balls.

Manta rays are fishes, but 'fly' underwater li

Giant kelp is the longest seaweed in the world. One leaf, called a frond, can be over 60 m long!

giant birds. They can leap out of the water to heights of up to 2 metres.

Did You Know ?

Giant squid have eyes bigger than large frying pans.

A great white shark can swallow a dolphin whole.

An oarfish is as long as five table tennis tables.

Giant kelp grows in a seaweed forest under the ocean waves.

Female angler fish have a glow-in-the-dark fishing lure that attracts food.

Angler fish can cram enormous meals into their stretchy stomachs. They need to eat as much as possible in one meal, as food is hard to find in the dark ocean depths.

Body bits

From huge horns and claws
to enormous tummies and tails,
the body bits of some animals
really are mega! Big horns and
claws are great for fighting
battles. Long tails are handy for
balancing, signalling or just
hanging on tight.

A rhino's horns are made of hairs packed tightly together.

This male giant
seahorse has a big
belly because hundreds of baby
seahorses are inside a pouch on
the front of his body.

A white
rhino's huge front
horn can grow up to twice
as long as a person's arm.
This horn looks big, but they
can be even bigger!

The front claws
of a mantid shrimp
shoot out, in a blow
with the impact of a bullet,
to stun their prey.

Male ring-tails spread scent on their tails and have stink fights!

TRUE
or
FALSE

*The bill of the Australian
pelican is as long as a person's arm?*

*An elephant's trunk has more
than 100 muscles?*

*Baby rhinos have soft, floppy
horns when they are born?*

?

Answers on page 22

Did You Know ?

A new baby seahorse is
only as big as your little fingernail.

The biggest Japanese spider crab
was 3.7 m across its front claws.

A toucan's big bill is made
of keratin, like your
fingernails.

The ring-tailed lemur's
long, stripey tail is important
for balance. The lemur also
lifts its tail high in the air to
signal to other ring-tails.

15

A crab can give you a nasty
nip with its big pincers! Crabs
also use them for picking up,
cutting and crushing their food.
Some male crabs wave one big
claw to threaten rival males
and impress a mate.

Sharp, wavy edges to grip and cut slippery food.

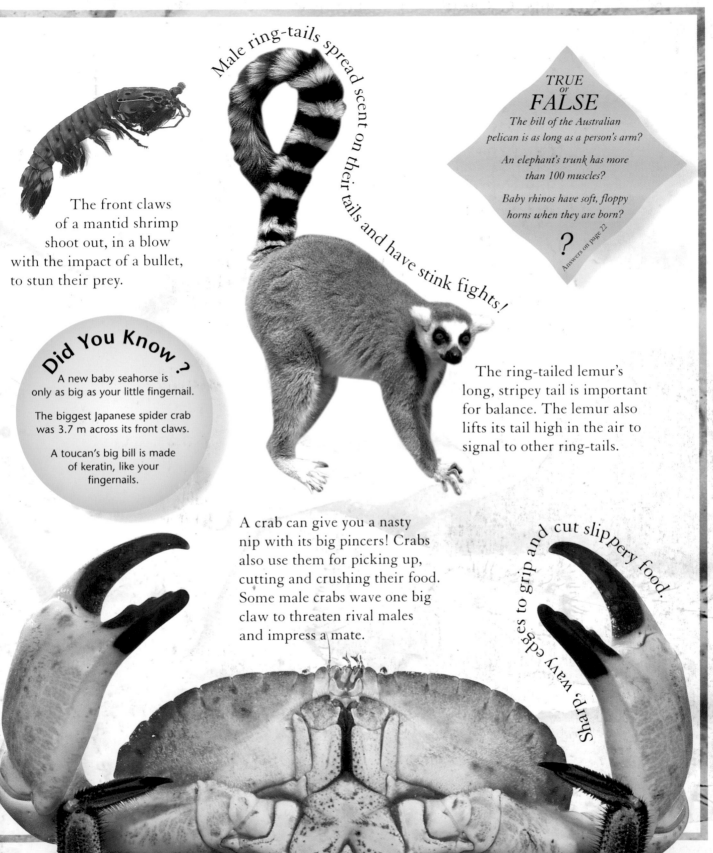

Eggs and baby birds

Big birds lay big eggs. The world's biggest bird - the ostrich - lays the biggest egg of any living bird. The largest bird's egg ever was laid by a giant flightless bird called *Aepyornis*. It was as big as 220 chicken's eggs! An ostrich's egg is only as big as 24 chicken's eggs.

ostrich egg

tawny owl egg

Fluffy down feathers keep these baby tawny owls warm by trapping warm air like a feather duvet.

16

Baby tawny owls are born blind, helpless and covered in down feathers. They leave the nest after about five weeks, but their parents keep feeding them for about three months.

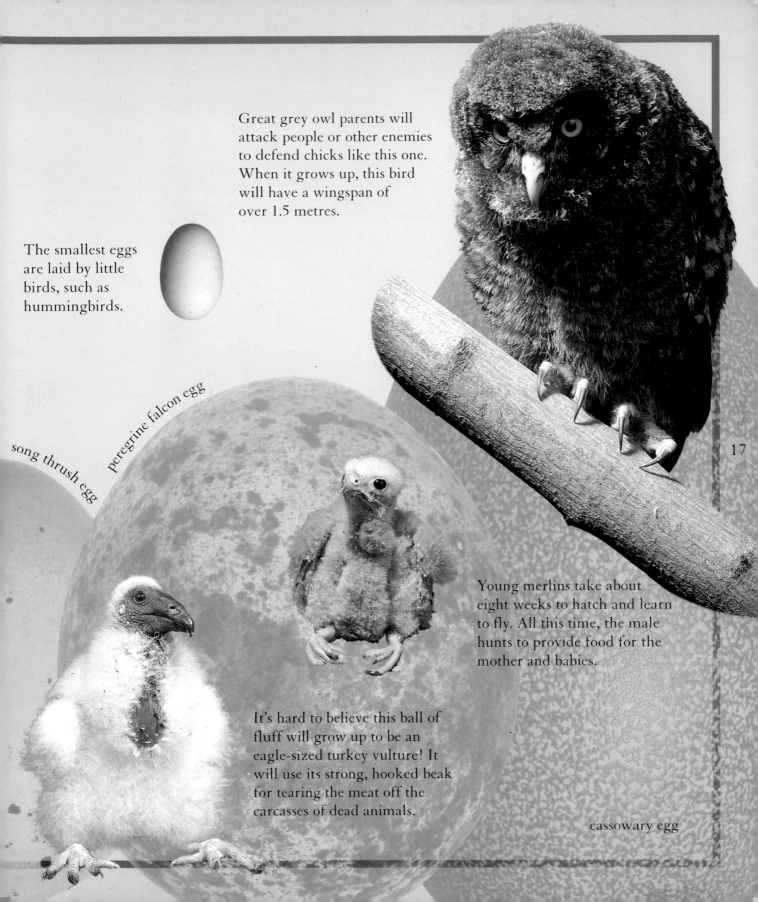

Great grey owl parents will attack people or other enemies to defend chicks like this one. When it grows up, this bird will have a wingspan of over 1.5 metres.

The smallest eggs are laid by little birds, such as hummingbirds.

peregrine falcon egg

song thrush egg

17

Young merlins take about eight weeks to hatch and learn to fly. All this time, the male hunts to provide food for the mother and babies.

It's hard to believe this ball of fluff will grow up to be an eagle-sized turkey vulture! It will use its strong, hooked beak for tearing the meat off the carcasses of dead animals.

cassowary egg

Minibeasts

Minibeasts are limited in size because their hard external skeletons can only support light weights. Their breathing systems would also not work if their bodies were larger. Even so, some mini-beasts have grown to giant sizes. Here are some of the biggest.

Giant millipedes look fierce, but they eat only dead plants.

Millipedes from tropical countries sometimes grow into giants, because it is always warm and there's plenty of food.

This giant wasp measures about 12 cm from one wingtip to another.

The tarantula hawk wasp is the largest wasp in the world. Females sting large spiders so they are still alive but cannot move. They lay eggs on the paralysed spiders, so the young wasps can eat fresh spider meat when they hatch!

The helicopter damselfly is the world's largest damselfly, with a wingspan of 19 cm. It swoops down into forest clearings on its fine wings, and plucks spiders from their webs.

This Australian Hercules moth has the largest wingspan of any insect alive today - 28 cm! Some insects that lived on Earth millions of years ago had much larger wingspans, up to 70 cm.

The female Queen Alexandra's birdwing butterfly is the largest butterfly in the world. It is also one of the rarest.

These extraordinary horns are longer than the beetle's body!

The longest beetles in the world are Hercules beetles from Central and South America. Males can be up to 19 cm long.

Micromarvels

When you zoom in really close to ordinary things with a microscope, a surprising new world opens up before your eyes. Insects look like aliens from space, dust is full of monsters and salt seems to be made up of enormous rocks!

Dust mites munch away at the bits of skin that flake off our bodies. They think skin flakes are really delicious!

Let's hope we never meet a house fly this size! You can see the many lenses that make up each compound eye. There are also three simple eyes on top of its head. The fly smells with the antennae between its eyes, and tastes with its feet.

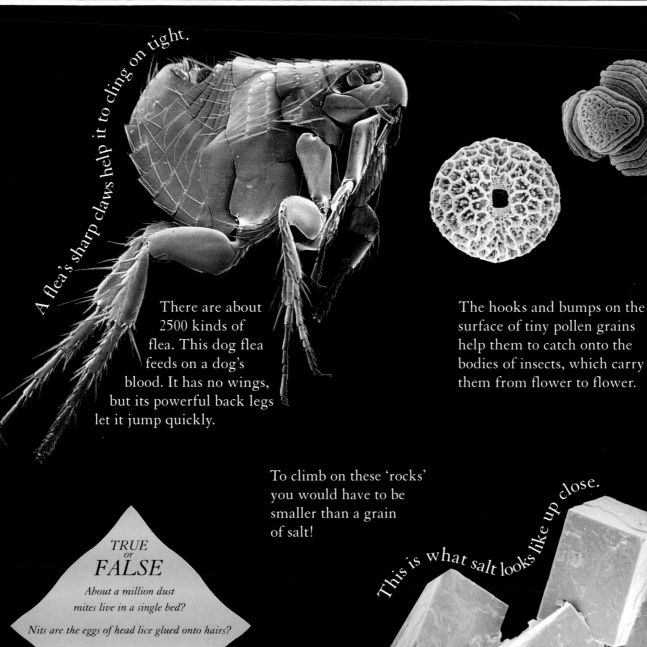

A flea's sharp claws help it to cling on tight.

There are about 2500 kinds of flea. This dog flea feeds on a dog's blood. It has no wings, but its powerful back legs let it jump quickly.

The hooks and bumps on the surface of tiny pollen grains help them to catch onto the bodies of insects, which carry them from flower to flower.

21

To climb on these 'rocks' you would have to be smaller than a grain of salt!

TRUE
or
FALSE

About a million dust mites live in a single bed?

Nits are the eggs of head lice glued onto hairs?

Hayfever is caused by dust mites?

?

Answers on page 22

This is what salt looks like up close.

Index

22

True or False answers

Being big
★ False, a blue whale is only half as long as
  an Olympic pool.
★ True, they grow up to 36 m.
★ False, the fungus can grow even bigger,
  up to 30 cm across.

Giant killers
★ False, this shark eats plankton.
★ True, these bears are fast!
★ False, anacondas live in South America, and elephants
  live in Africa and Asia.

Body bits
★ False, but it is as long as an adult's lower arm,
  from elbow to fingertip.
★ False, it has only 6 muscles.
★ False, they have no horns at all.

Micromarvels
★ True, unfortunately!
★ True.
★ False, hayfever is caused by pollen.